MW01259834

DESERT JOURNAL

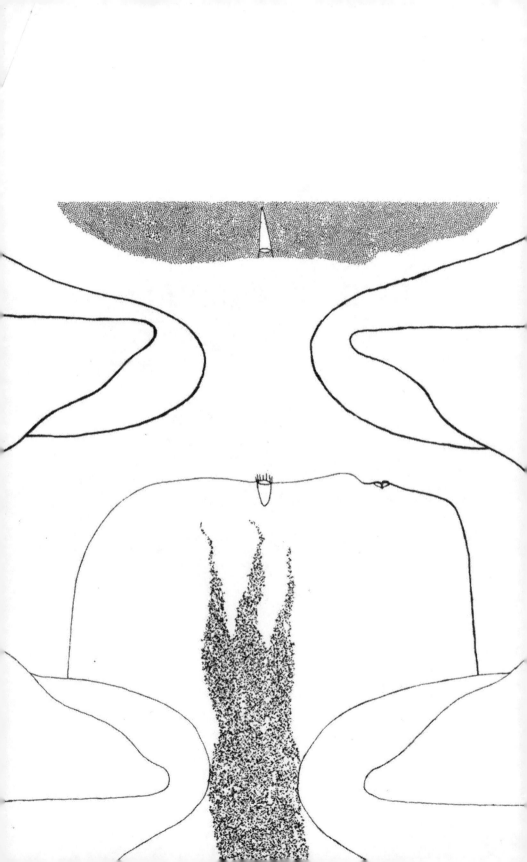

DESERT JOURNAL

ruth weiss

drawings
Paul Blake

Trembling Pillow Press — New Orleans — 2012

DESERT JOURNAL by ruth weiss

Trembling Pillow Press
New Orleans, LA
ISBN-13: 978-0-9790702-7-3
Copyright © 2012 ruth weiss
Covers and drawings © 2012 Paul Blake
First Edition, 1977 (Good Gay Poets, Boston)

All Rights Reserved. No part of this book may be reproduced
in any form without permission from the publisher with
the exception of brief passages cited or for educational
purposes. Reproduction for commercial use is prohibited
except by permission of the author.

Typesetting and Design: Megan Burns and Geoff Munsterman
Cover: Dave Brinks
Author Photo: Christopher Felver

DESERT JOURNAL was first published in 1977 in hardback
and paperback editions by Good Gay Poets, Boston. The only
changes made to the text are the addition of page numbers
and a table of contents.

Trembling
Pillow
PRESS

http://tremblingpillowpress.com

Contents

for all artists who work from their inner truth

to keep the faith that their work will find

its way to be shared

you are entering a certain desert

like stones or bones
marking sand

flame & cloud
things with wings
call your number
read your day
see if it talks to you alone
like stone or bone
in sand

other days
other ways ———

FIRST DAY

the tables sat end on end
they were dropping into the cavity of mouth
slowly
as slow as speed
one would not notice
only if one watched closely
they would drop one by one
yet they would remain the same number
never one less
never one more

NEVERMORE quoth the bird ————
the fable-bird
and the tables kept dropping
it does not matter whether
there is an ash-tray on each one of them
or anythingelse
whatever is on one
is on each of them

bird-droppings
and then it was in the desert
knew not how it got there
kept on flying to find direction
alone now
but still with feet
could land
i'm in indian territory
terrified it cried
i'm a kangaroo-bird
carry my own pouch
either sex
or both
what is the hermaphroditic fact?

no name to touch
to touch has no name

went loving the enemy more

only friend is end
the cut instead of curve

to underline what one already knows
now undermine the how
how it was
how it was!

will be
the will to be
must cut all friend
the trend must curve
as rainbow does its arc a circle

all animal lives against
makes its own on the loan of its extension
aura
possibility of become

to lend is not a friend

went loving the enemy more

sent by what is below
to blow one down
or make a crown of thorns
the roses know that story

or bring one over

RED ROVER
RED ROVER
come over!

no oasis
no camel or kangaroo
no pouch of one's own

went loving the enemy more

the mores asunder
as thunder BEFORE lightning struck
did anyone count?
the seconds all felt the duel
though none of them would ever die for it

not being first has its compensation
do you REALLY WANT YOUR COMPENSATION
lightning struck
DO YOU REALLY WANT YOUR COMPENSATION?

sate
ate all the tables
as they dropped one by one

one plus one is two
two plus two is four
four is no more
(singular of mores)
than now

the law always behind
where it is safe
to have a behind
or vast past
do not wiggle
do not giggle
THIS IS SERIOUS!

and the first day
is the worst day
in the desert

they tell one to make a fast last
slow ——— like a dirty bird

SECOND DAY

one has to throw it all away
notes ——— numbers
all the references
even the reverence of nothing
mirror ——— memory
all hinges
swinging doors to possibility
even heat ——— cold
the backs of strangers
even cold ——— heat
the front familiar
even evil sweet

there is a point
where the last rescue
of love is possible
there is that point of lasting
the tall love calls
a cat shadow
on a wall
and is it a or the
or is it singularly plural?
who are you to say
how s should be placed
if?

THERE IS NO EVIL
ONLY RESTLESSNESS!

sometimes
someone
quite blond
and black
speaks out
like smoke
spoke without
knowing words
speaks out

the wheel of words
are left to the rule of the city
she will play
because
just because
no cause
no justice
not even how

but to know
is never to reap

to love is a yes
is a kind ———
is not kind
is low
and someone will leap in
no year

the girl who doesn't drink
the girl who doesn't think
is the girl who
once
is was once
yes!

who are you to say
a or the?

THIRD DAY

it is wet   it is cold
each step causes a ravine
the only way not to be
the shiver within the flood
is to become one with the stream
NO!
not one with the stream
TO BE THE STREAM!
not to scream
TO BE THE SCREAM!
from so deep within
that even the word SOURCE
is lost to its cause
thus to cause the source

SOUR SAUCE
SOUR SAUCE
MARINATE THIS LIFE
WITHOUT SEEMING CAUSE

VICE HAS LOST ITS SHARP
SHARP HAS LOST ITS SPICE
VICE HAS LOST ITS SHARP
HARP HAS LOST ITS STRING
STRING HAS LOST ITS WING
HARP HAS LOST ITS SPRING
SPRING HAS LOST ITS SING
WING HAS LOST ITS BIRD
BIRD HAS LOST ITS TURD
VICE HAS LOST ITS SPICE

AND TURD ON THE THIRD
DAY HOPE AS SPICE THE NIGHT
NIGHT HAS LOST ITS FIGHT
TO BE THE ONE UNKNOWN
WANT TO BE
AS SOWN THE SEED
THE NEED ———

ONLY SOME BIRD
STILL HAS THE TURD
TO

only one who will still scream
NOT STILL THE SCREAM ———

the still in the ozark hill
where the government man goes
in all directions
not having his own direction
unable to ask
only to question ————

only a lone coyote
in flight from beast
in his image
in flight from man
who flies from his scream
in flight from man
who will only hear
the cry of too many birds
falling turds
calling time

only one who will still scream ———
one who wouldn't even
consider the government man less
than those who possess
and consider direction
of importance

this is the wind
the wind could be considered
the wind could be considered strong
this is the hill i cannot talk about
it's a hill
a hill
a hill
not a cliff
not a cliff at all
nothing as strong as that
just a hill against the wind

it was here ten years ago that ———
or ten million

a way of saying time
which always resists the saying of it

is this the table?
we are not ready
it hurts
it hurts
it hurts
so much to be said
and nothing

a coyote dies at sunset
in flight from beast
in his image
in flight from man
who flies from his scream
in flight from man
who will only hear
the cry of too many birds
falling turds
calling time

a red dog named ZIMZUM
brings HOME a coyotes who SEES
the sunrise & DIES

red scum indian sun
no R in may june july august
so the sea demands its S

but a coyote with a capital S
is brought back to life in may
at sunrise
by a red dog named ZIMZUM
who ——— one year later
or one million
a way of saying time
which always resists the saying of it ———
stares into the sunset in august
every night
before dying

the last time he smiled

FOURTH DAY

nine lives
one cat-step at a time
each one more pain
each one more easy
each one deeper

breaking ground in the desert
is ridiculous
seems pointless
the desert remains AS IS

SAPPHO
beside herself
is poem
short words
long steps
cruel nights
sharp dawn & blue
a she-cat
seven spots on her white belly
a dancer
her gyrations hidden generations
it was thought
she'd never had a litter before

there were six
mixed as is usual
she left to their thin fate
on an invisible thread herself

perhaps she still lives
on her thinning line

the six never knew a name
though they were all promised
a destination
and took some human blood
in their wake

it was tuesday
OCHO was born
on the day the lovers
thought their morn
but turned them mourning
before the summer-sun set

OCHO locked out
on a tuesday
born in the eighth month
the eighth cat in the house
with an eight so white
on a black belly

perhaps he still lives
in somebody's eighth house

MONK nine
almost named NUEVE
known as NUREYEV to someone else
danced on such strong paws
in careful abandon
breaking all cat-rules
letting love in
knowing it could never be ———
not from all previous experience

at one year
more than centuries old
let himself be born again

glass finer than sand
splintered on whatever stage
was chosen for him

black
so much like OCHO
so different
his markings a cunt on his belly
walking black with white
piano-keys color reversed
a monastery creature not celibate
that he-cat all love
allowing love in

the wind moves the kitchen-curtains
with his image
as he sits on the steps outside
the wind moves kitchen-curtain
his image gone
into the night

nine lives
one cat-step at a time
each one more pain
each one more easy
each one deeper

breaking ground in the desert
is ridiculous
seems pointless
the desert remains AS IS

back broken
broken back
the cat MONK
allows his belly
with cunt-markings
to be stroked
purring to death
BE NOT AFRAID
I AM READY
FOR THAT SEPARATION
THAT IS ONE

FIFTH DAY

one changes rooms
one changes buildings
one changes cities
one changes countries
one changes continents
planets

it is still the same universe
one's own

and the desert calls
over & over it calls
attuned one becomes comfortable
too late!
one is listening
for the sound that has stopped
point of no return

memory is a tree
burn dead leaves
leave not a single thought
to prey upon the present
girft the blooming
with fresh start

startle all the hidden demons
to release ———
to dance
and change
into their other shape

take over
each room
each building
each city
each country
each continent
all the planets

turn each & all
from the moment of recall
to the moment that IS NOW————
the desert
that by its very barren-ness
holds all possibles

a presence felt
not dared yet touched by sight
the eye withdrawn
yet curving imperceptibly
to encompass the possible
improbability of light

the way is always open
in the desert

what is this?
an oasis?

swarms sound
turns tangible
word colony a colon
two dots like eyes
each dot an eye
out of the crowd it flies
straight as the fabled crow
across to the one marked NOW
on entering

LEPERS REPEL
LEPER REPELS
REPEL
LEPER
within yourselves
it spells
that swarm sound
INSOMNIA   INSOMNIA
with so much sand around
could not a grain
pass in-between
and make my friction
INSOMNIA
a pearl?

FOREVER CHANGES
rooms
buildings
cities
countries
the planet

startle all the hidden demons
to release ———
to dance
and change
into their other shape

startle all the hidden demons
to release ———
to dance
and change
into their other shape

a sand-painting
a sand-bird spreading its sand-wings
will it fly
hard-driving dawn?

SIXTH DAY

the sixth day considers itself
a sand-mound
beyond all others ———
makes its thought
mountain upon mountain

the desert considers nothing
it is the justice
of six points
connected

and pushed into shape
by whomever wills it

the arrow points its direction
the arrow finds its mark
even if seeming intention
is not struck
like fuck
it happens wherever

the weight
and the wait
in balance
where all gathers

no guarantee the return
no guarantee

facts
like fuck
changing in its veritus

the look familiar
the look stranger
the look familiar
the look stranger
the look familiar
the look stranger
look now
won kool
look now
won kool
look now
won kool
look a stranger
look a familiar
look a stranger
look a familiar
look a stranger
look a familiar

facts
like fuck
changing in its veritus

the arrow points its direction
the arrow finds its mark
even if seeming intention
is not struck
like fuck
it happens wherever

the desert is fine
it conjures all places
this is considered mirage
ageless
without mirror
it is considered illusion ———
the pure-point where all gathers

one dreams of the tree
another of the sea
one dreams of the root
another of the foot
one dreams of the hand
another of the sand
that makes its thought
mountain upon mountain

the desert considers nothing
it is the justice
of six points
connected

where did one find granite
to stone
his herd into a shape
without guarantee?

the archer & the slinger
the parcher & the singer
wings of stone
the desert grinds its tone
upon the bone of earth
and the sixth day
is betwixt creation
and the light

the desert considers nothing
it is the justice
of six points
connected

and pushed into shape
by whomever wills it

the bright hand on the bare door
the bare hand on the bright door ————

SEVENTH DAY

where is hawaii?
what is hawaii?
a sound of wave against wave
slapping
where the woodrose grows
sand & foam
mother & father
allusion to sea
illusion of ocean
a sound of wave against wave
slapping

KAHLUAH
1 quart brandy
1 pint boiling water
2 cups unrefined sugar
2 ounces instant coffee
1 whole vanilla bean
mix sugar & coffee
add boiling water
dissolve ———

i must acknowledge the fact
that nothing is permanent

let cool add brandy
store in dark place

i got you backwards
in my mind

tie a string to
vanilla bean & drop

a sound of wave against wave
slapping

remove after thirty days

a sound of wave against wave
slapping

and all the old doors were open
until i tried them
but if old ———
and if sweethearts
with young faces
and old hearts
brush their dusty tales
on ground floors
fine dust
like fuck
and god
and metaphysical
and right
and wrong
and all the other
dangerous
words
that make a floor
saw dust
like sand
fine like desert-sand ———

where is hawaii?
what is hawaii?
where is the arc-angel?
where is satan?
conversing no doubt
deep in conversation
each to the other
each is the other
no doubt
PAISLEY
no pictures
PLEASE!

just now a face i knew ————
but no!
on the journey
the same faces over & over
NOW to go behind the face ————
one's own face

AND ON THE SEVENTH DAY
THE DARKNESS SAW ITSELF!

what is the question?
she said & died

the stranger behind the face
one's own face ———— smirks
don't you know you've changed?
still at the old doors?

and on the seventh day
a clown turned mute
to play his flute

DIE EINSAMKEIT IST NOTH
DOCH SEI NUR NICHT GEMEIN
SO KANNST DU UEBERALL
IN EINER WUESTEN SEIN

solitude is need
but be not mean
thus you be anywhere
as in a desert

face
the face
know the face
and know the face
solitude is need
but do not stoop to greed
thus you be in all places
and know the face that ALL FACES
and know the face that IS ALL FACES
solitude is need   solitude is need ———

AND ON THE SEVENTH DAY
the toe of the foot of the leg
struck sand cast shadow
of the dark archer

AND ON THE SEVENTH DAY
ALL LIGHT!!!

a sound of wave against wave
slapping

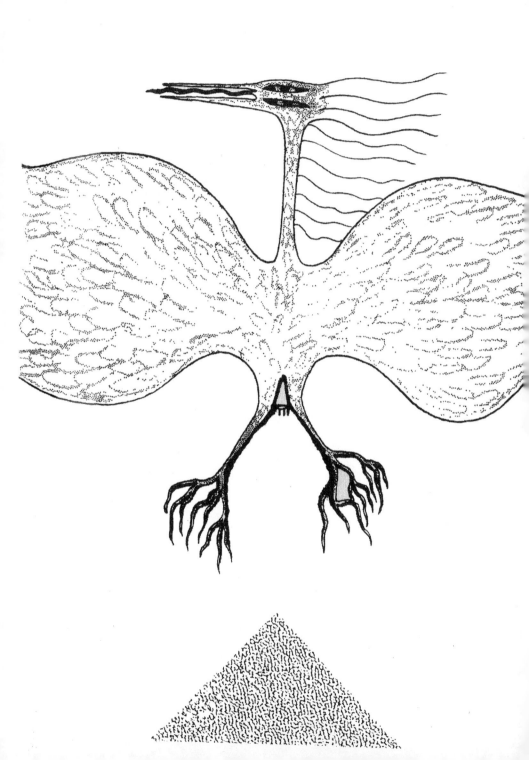

EIGHTH DAY

we can't be friends
but we don't have to be enemies

the crab-witch
becomes
sorcerer
atlantis reascends in mars
the violence spends itself
letting go

only the fire-bird perched
on peak of pyramid
beak still open to soul-stars
on set wet claws

the myths are true
as are you
whoever the you may be
at the moment of telling
the teller of them
the last one to believe

flash the energy stretches
a clown-bird destruction
to its wing-tip
wing & whoosh
who wants any part
of that kind of flying?

the desert is fatigue
the desert is all living organism
in the face
of continual annihilation

the desert is all myth
and all true
as are you
whoever the you may be
at the moment of telling
the teller of them
the last one to believe

there may be an open door
that is really locked
there could be a lock on another
that is really open

only the desert
being vast & slow
fast like so much sand
could conjure doors & locks
in open space

only the desert
where the fire-bird perched
on peak of pyramid
beak still open to soul-stars
on set wet claws

fingers from hands
clenched yet pointing
to black night
glistening stars
one black dog
no owner in sight
or out of vision ———

the visionary black dog
only guard
not messenger yet
is learning too
as you
who must follow
the fingers from hands
clenched yet pointing

there are no stars left
to right
wrong imagined
only the myths are true
as are you
whoever the you may be
at the moment of telling
the teller of them
the last one to believe

we can't be friends
but we don't have to be enemies

the crab-witch
becomes
sorcerer
atlantis went down
in a wall of water
and the fire
breathes
breathes
burning breath
sand
life & death ———
one ball

NINTH DAY

no animals allowed!
sign of the times
no animals allowed inside

wuz talkin' to meself
and you know what
wuz talkin' to god
do you believe that?

wanted you to smile
so i'd find out
what day it wuz
do you believe that?

sand the old man
meant it
every word
every fuckin' word!

KING TUT went PUT PUT
and all the people went tut tut
sputter & PUT PUT the train
steam whistling down the track
and we rolled
how we rolled
in the cold
sharing blanket
and covering the countryside

the landscape is each other
each dwelling smaller than life
size to fit no more imagination
caught as meant

sand the old man
meant it
every word
every fuckin' word!

one thing she's found out
she doesn't have to suffer anymore

flicker the light
was it day or is it night?
was it forest or is it plain?
was it mist or is it rain?

the track twists
we are thrown
as grains of sand
anonymous as animals
the train rolls on
upon the track

there are gentle ones
crossing the desert
carrying the great violence
earning the right
to disperse
the great violence

there are clumsy ones
caught in the cities
carrying the great violence
earning the right
to disperse

it could be a train
it could be a plane
the steam could be jet
or better yet ———

the landscape is each other
each dwelling smaller than life
larger than strife
size to fit no more imagination
caught as meant

sand the old man
meant it
every word
every fuckin' word!

it could be a train
it could be a plane
the steam could be jet
or better yet
only a wheel

reel the universe!
real as scratching one's back
upon the track
like an animal

it is a hard thing
for an animal
to break habit

comic-strip ———
spill of one-number clocks
upright flowers
imaginable animals ———
caption:
HOW MANY TIMES
HAVE I TOLD YOU
TO PUT YOUR ILLUSIONS AWAY
WHEN THROUGH PLAYING!

the landscape is each other
each dwelling smaller than life
TUT TUT no more imagination
caught as meant

TENTH DAY

one invents a place to be ———
a place that is
precisely what one is
aura to core

taut cord
taut as in tight
blocking the light

snap loose!
use any ruse
universe laughter holds the fuse

on the stage of change
each role a full range
that one must play out
sometime

sometimes
one walks a quiet path
to enter chaos

sometimes
one seeks the nomad
to find the self
in no mad land ———
only a pasture

sometimes
some times are drops of water
in the desert

the place is unimportant
until called
given a name
put into a setting
become responsibility

concept of color change
translating one's responses

who was the child
still unguiled
clutching toys from another place?

what is that face
of a whole human race
that gazes through one's eyes?

who is that one mad
breaking the staff
that served as guide?

silhouette
sunset or dawn
born to die & born once more
gouging the lie from its core

hell picked up
carried piggy-back
up a solitary hill ———
a hill of sand
once solid land
now a wind-drift
shifting

the place is unimportant
until called
given a name
put into a setting
become responsibility

where is that name
that was?
now loose as a toy
and as telling
to tell one story
once more

once upon a time
a ball of fire
once upon a time
a part set loose in orbit ———
toy of the whole ———

unimportant
until called
given a name
put into a setting
become responsibility

aura to core
a child
the face
mad one
silhouette
sunset through dawn
and dawn once more
gouges the lie from its core

ELEVENTH DAY

through the swirl & mist of sand
appears a figure
in dots
as if of sand
it is the same figure as before
it is not the same
it is not the same one
it does not seem that way
it is another direction

suddenly
a structure
in the desert
story upon story
electric mass the windows
mathematic glitter
in the noon-desert sun

night
one light
in the story
in the structure
in the desert
one flight before the top

through the swirl & mist of sand
appears a figure
in dots
as if of sand ———
vanishes as if again
contacts
like an eye
lost in done & die
no color left in the sky
blue bright
reflection
thought black
lack of light

now is then
who when
divides it all?

it all
goes up in smoke
poke the embers
the ashes left
have to do it again

story upon story
a structure of lies

desert take all

it all
goes up in smoke
poke the embers
the ashes left
have to do it again

desert take all

fall or rise
a story dies

a sea without fish
a desert without wish
it trickles through
one's fingers burning

see red the stars the day the sun
in the desert
thought black
lack of light

stars bright
trickling through
one's fingers burning

shake cold!
bake old!
burn hot or cold!
turn cold or hot!
but never look back
like wife of lot

through the swirl & mist of sand
appears a figure
in dots
as if of sand
it is the same figure as before
it is not the same
it is not the same one
it does not seem that way
it is another direction

who went that way?
who went what way?

swirl-dots
pearls of sand
land or sea
who sees?

went to the bottom of the sea
it was said
there is no bottom
went to the top of the sky
it was said
there is no why

who dare to cry
at all?

it all
goes up in smoke
poke the embers
the ashes left
have to do it again

who dares to cry?

now is then
who when
divides a wild red moon
settling closer
to the angle of the sun?

see red the stars the day

who
in
what
desert?

TWELFTH DAY

solid statements
promises
meant as rock
rock crumbles
the desert a sea of rocks

go with thirst
the desert will slake it
do not ask how
go with thirst

lizard or ant
turn into any
to become many
it is easy then
the desert

but if you stay alone
be prepared to be stone
like a human being only

a well
it is abandoned
it will not give water
fly off the handle
it makes no difference
it will not give water ———
only teaches the wanderer
to handle the wanderer
turns what is left by man
into hope abandoned ———
a random stop in the desert

meant as rock
promises
solid statements
rock crumbles
the desert a sea of rocks

solemn the night
the desert was bright
clouds & light
a moment ago

now sound bound
springs to the well
sings to the stone
prepared to be alone
like a human being only

stars in the well
solemn the night

promises
solid statements
meant as rock
the desert a sea of rocks
rock crumbles

went as a lizard
went as an ant
the desert handles
no more than can't

recant now
it is still time
all the easy demons
want to play

SAY! GIRL!
SAAY!
who are you
to put it all down
stay alone
become stone
like a human being only?

THIRTEENTH DAY

wheels flash in the desert
dawn floods red & round
raw begins this day
in the desert

fumed from ghost & silver-white
spokes turning the night before
spoke the chief & entourage
wordless leaves
dapple-breeze the night
no more rage
sage-sweet
bright right

wheels flash
crash sand
flies dream to scream
the stream apart
each grain

all pain
is all what one
meant only
upon oneself

like the elf running
lightly
brightly only
on the path just yet darted
charted
in the light of a night ———
the night there is no moon

soon
one sez to oneself
of elf
run light
sage-sweet
bright right

the spider is a wheel
is an eye
lie against lie
each spoke against the universe
threading the universe
from its universal slime

lucid wild & lurid
the crime of the spider
is the crime
of wider
and wider
and wider
contained within
the universal thread

riled it turns threat
weave wordless leaves

raw begins this day
in the desert

sage-sweet
bright right

all pain
is all what one
meant only
upon oneself

all pain
is all what one
meant only
upon oneself

wheels
in the desert
flash
floods red
round day

no more rage
in the light of a night ————
the night there is no moon

soon the spider
an eye against eye
lie to lie
spokes against
and for this universe
against the universal slime

FOURTEENTH DAY

prickly pear
prickly hair
cold wind sand singing
whiplash gash eyes
pain insane the hidden lies

fine hair to fate
unrelate
no more pickled memory
break the jars
instead of pickling for winter

prickly pear
the desert puts up no nonsense
the desert puts up with no nonsense
the desert *puts down*
what should not be done
the desert puts *down*
what must be done

quickly prepare
leave quickly
proud air
rare abandon
the journey is day by day
as soup of the day
not a soupçon of hope
soup's on
but one goes
in the throes
without trace
without grace

the prickly pear
only grows in the desert

each day is a present to oneself
each day is a why
a fork in the road
but there is no road
in the desert

they collided in an arc

where is the ark?
asked the lark
where is the road?
asked the toad
egad said the crab
it's a trapezoid

memory too long ago
said the elephant
and the bull brushed bruised horns
against the prickly pear

paradox
said the ox

a sand-flea flees
he's seen too much already
i'm ready
screams the ostrich
paradox
said the ox

knock upon a rock with grief
screeches the bird
known as a thief
litter glitter!
bitter flitter!
nods the elephant
that gold is an old story
and rocks grind down
in the desert

the crab is looking for the sea
the toad is looking for the road
the lark looking for the ark
is only after his song ———
while the bull brushes bruised horns
against the prickly pear

break the jars
instead of pickling for winter

glass-splinters
grind down like rocks
in the desert
ground down
down a mirage

paradox
said the ox

down said the geese
in formation
up said the geese
in formation
there's no more
to be learned here

prickly pear
prickly hair
cold wind sand singing
whiplash

is it a road?
is it a boat?
egad said the crab
it's a trapezoid

FIFTEENTH DAY

point-period-dot
the desert-wanderer comes to a stop
the journey a line begun
as a dot
as a dot become

recall makes vanish
a dervish-dance
deviled to spin one to a point
where quests & discovery
end at a period
that lasts until the line of the journey
forms once more

a stranger familiar
crushes something into the palm
the hand becomes a tree
there is shade & fruit
ripe drooping
fingers stretch to enclose
its universe
free
sounds fill what was vacuum
cradling release

rolled into space
struck ground
the body vanishes
still tangible

another body follows
strikes
vanishes
still tangible

other bodies follow
strike
vanish
still tangible

the bodies the fruit of the tree
raucous & ripe
turning spirit

stop!
there is still need
for the desert

point-period-dot
all life turns
to its cell once more
sound shrieks to a roar
to a line as fine
as the root of one hair
spun to its begun
all life turns
to its cell once more ———
its original prison

a finger
a hand stretched forth
stretches
touches land
vanishes
turns prism
the hand a prism
its tangible turned light

laugher of the universe
no trace of its begun
not a point-period-dot
no start
no stop
laugher startled
startling the universe
all is laughter

i laugh
you laugh
it laughs

we cry
you cry
they cry

tears harsh as grains of sand
it rains upon the land
the desert is not barren
at this point

this period will last
as long as the first
word heard
sound formed
from the dot
of its shriek
roar to its line
fine as the root of one hair
on one hand
reaching

SIXTEENTH DAY

one could be so close
after all the dark spells
sent upon one
spent
dispelled ————
after all the hell-bent hopes
bent to unfamiliar
after all
it is only how
not why or when
it is then
that it could be so close

oh the gypsy woman
oh the gypsy woman comes
sing the chorus of children free
as they watch her
as they watch me
from their opening
steps gleaming
as they watch her
as they watch me
mount the steps
from the abyss

bright things
rings the canyon
bright things
rings on fingers
desert-wings struck still

is it stone?
is it bone?
is it a throne for bird or beast?
does the sun rise in the east?
at least there is no chart
for the heart to set its at to

once upon
a nun on words
went wings
canyon-rings
to reach the human screech
the boundless of the beast
the soundless four-foot tone
known as coyote

coyote
liar
teller of all truths
tooth in check
beckons
to his other self
left loose & toothless
by coyote

once upon
a nun on words
crossed convent border
line & dot
to set the heart
where it's at upon

once upon
one could be so close
after all the dark spells
and hell-bent hopes
slope to the east
sent to the sun

what is this?
another game?

i would like
to make a call
to no-place!

SEVENTEENTH DAY

to move across one's plane
slowly from point to point
weaving for a focus
as far as reached
an eye-flash
a contact
return for confirmation
to one's starting-point
the equi-distant triangle complete

one's starting-point
slowly from one's focus
to strike as far as reached
to flash across its equal thought
return for confirmation
to one's starting-point
the equi-distant triangle complete

two inverted
equi-distant
triangles
touch
to form a square

there was no warning at all!
there was all warning needed!
there was no warning at all!

there was all warning needed!
there was no warning at all!
there was all warning needed!

so much warning
one was lulled by its constancy
when it struck
all seemed surprised
no one was surprised

it was as sudden
as if it had always been
it was too late
it was too early
it happened

fear is the nightmare not remembered!

REMEMBER THE NIGHTMARE!
REMEMBER THE NIGHTMARE!
REMEMBER THE NIGHTMARE!

nightmare is remember
nightmare is remember
nightmare is remember

AND THEN IS GONE!

baby we must dance!
baby where to dance?
baby we must dance!

baby where to dance?
baby we must dance!
baby where to dance?

TO DANCE RIGHT NOW!

the rock under the cloud
the cloud under the rock
the rock under the sea

the sea over the rock
the rock over the cloud
the cloud over the rock

though the earth be of the ox
still the earth is paradox
PARADOX IS PARADOX

this is the day that
could never be done
this is the day that
must all ways be ONE

seventeen is one plus seven
heaven help!
INFINITY!

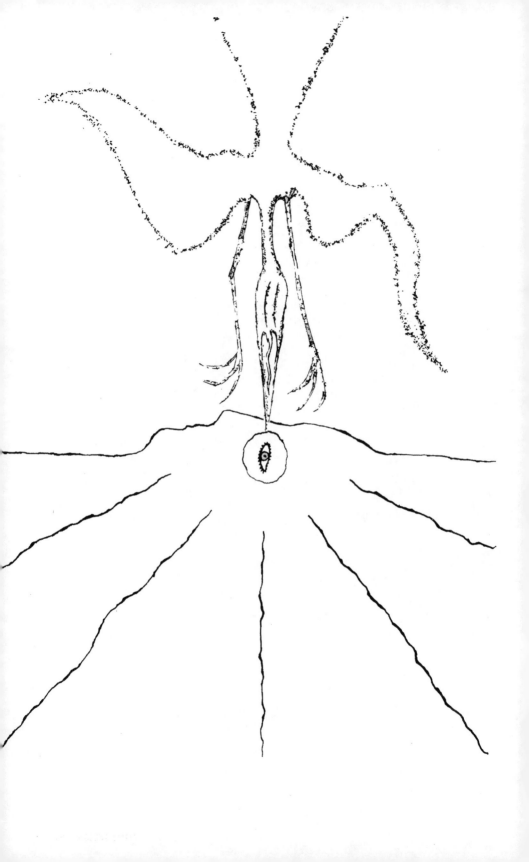

EIGHTEENTH DAY

a feast!   a feast!
to celebrate the beast
raging in the winter of the soul

fire the tapers
for outrageous capers
the odds against light
should tempt the demons to attend
the impossible dance
is within the reach of each
and the outcast chants commence:

AKASAAD
RAKATUM
ECCOSA
FATANO
KAMA HO
HOLOKA
SAKAMA
AKASAAD
RAKATUM

KAPATA
SALANO
TONASA
HARATO
ULITA
ULITUM

no chant is chance

the impossible chance
is within the reach of each

SU-SU-SU
NOW IS THE TIME TO MEND
SPLIT ENDS

the whole within
holy holy
descend with broken wing slowly

momma momma why do i cry?
because you're still i
because you say momma
because you say die

a wish is no more than made
no more a maid
having once laid

ugly ugly ugly duckling
fucking the old woman
on a bank of sand
seeming in sleep
smiling deep
young boys swarming
a bank of sand

the whole within
holy holy
descend with broken wing slowly

to be boy
to be eye
to be treaded from the sky

each strong touch a weakening
not to shrink from
to meet all the way
till meeting becomes
circled eye

SU-SU-SU

split-end-antic
flicker as in no more
any one
to hang another up

THE HANGED MAN
A TAROT
miracle of easy-the-head
upside down

slow descent with broken wing

SU-SU-SU
NOW IS THE TIME TO MEND
SPLIT ENDS!

NINETEENTH DAY

sit
facing a mirror squarely
knees barely
touching its surface

at the vanishing point
of hearing
reverse
knees touching
from inside out

an onion skin
lies on the floor
torn laughing

an onion skin
lies on the floor
of the other side
torn laughing

a disk
flashes letters M-O-R-E
MORE
disk & letters one color ———
any color
symbol it into D-4

A for the one
who missed most
being bright lights

B for the next
who missed most
watching sun set

C for the third
who missed most
feel of the sea

D for the last
who missed most

locked in granite
soul turning stone
disk burning letters L-E-S-S
LESS
disk & letters all color ———
all colors
symbol it into X-4

W for the one
who is
the double you

X for the next
who is
the one come

Y for the third
who is
just flown free

Z for the last
who is

looked at a clock
it struck four
looked at a clock
it struck three ———
both clocks striking
simultaneously

knew it was two

standard time
sidereal time
unreal time
and a good good time
was had by all
made one laugh
made one cry

knew it as two
knew it as one

if that is a way
out of the desert
who's left to answer
for all the folly?

FOLLY FLY PIE & SU CITY SU
us in the city
as i in the desert
pure to receive
all association
new association
without association ———
the purpose of the desert

a disk with letters L-M-N-O
letters no word
disk & letters no color
color of one
symbol it into
LOVE
MUST
NOW
OHM!

TWENTIETH DAY

and what of evil?

THERE IS NO EVIL
THE ONLY EVIL IS TO DENY LIFE!

d.h. lawrence ———

diane whispering
that the devil's strongest weapon
is to convince
he doesn't exist ———

so much horizon
on the desert ———

debauch ———
a desire for ———
a desert cactus
with tenacity itself as root
when it blooms ———
irresistible

an angel guards
each act of debauch ———
as long as one follows it through
let there be hesitation
and the devil wins the move
d as in damn
evil as in everyone

PROCRASTINATION!
it will not
it wills not
to let go
pounces each chance
the battered seeds
the scattered seed
the need will out

at that most unexpected moment ———
when wind hurling itself
most hurting fist & blindful
sand in eyes
a brown dirty paw the beast
no eye more sad
than that of the beast
the longing for
angel-wing caress

at that very moment ———
very
no more ugly word
in the english language
peaches & cream nun eulogia
said over her seven-stepped collar ———

verily & in truth
at that very moment ———
walking would be good for you
a calculation step by step ———
webbed back
1930 berlin
the circus masquerade
the last party
only a hitler could stop
only a devil could glee with hesitation
mommy would spike the punch
and get lost
mommy would have a good time
and lie on the floor
like the little girl she ———
and they were all there
and all kinds of things would go on
the circus masquerade
each one to perform in the arena
wild & wilder ———

the wind the wild desert wind
the battered seeds
the scattered seed
the need will out
a desert cactus
with tenacity itself as root
memory of all that death
the only thing to ease that pain
IS THAT I TOO WILL DIE SOMEDAY!

she didn't get the job
singing in the downstairs ———
little blond sally
sallied out
to make this world
the clubowner slobbering cigar
two-time loser on young girls
she was a young girl
pinned against the post
she didn't get the job

into it all
came LADY DAY
who throated the night after night
till throats
couldn't ever swallow again

diane whispering
sand in eyes
a brown dirty paw the beast
no eye more sad
than that of the beast
the longing for
angel-wing caress

a light that opens all doors
can never open its own

out-of-doors!
THE DESERT

TWENTY-FIRST DAY

the desert has as many facets
as the human heart
the desert is the squeeze
between each beat

to rise before midnight
to battle visitations
to face the unrelenting
procession through the night

through the black circle
the currents flick
their constant clash of forces

HAN GO NATSH AKAZUM TZEZERAK!

a coltrane record
just got stuck on
A LOVE SUPREME
A LOVE SUPREME
A LOVE SUPREME . . .

a toilet wall
flaunting ghost-erasures
gaunt & tall
calls
eternal soul
redeem your promise
in spite of night alone
and day on fire

the children stomping
on my door
this after-midnight door
without a key ———
a key without a turn

a flat slap back
into the dark reeling ————
screams too high-pitched
for human ear

pavilions of books
turn deaf-mute
turn butterflies
after the storm
not a flower moves

the earth-quake clown
is ringing the bells
of the village-church

NO MORE PROCRASTINATION!

delicate like his hands
he is moving
towards his own

it is not mine
it is not yours
it is only his
graveled multi-singular
each ring
to take him in
each ring
to take him once away
each ring
to bring him back again

to rise before midnight
to battle visitations
to face the unrelenting
procession through the night

through the black circle
the currents flick
their constant clash of forces

HAN GO NATSH AKAZUM TZEZERAK!

sounds like challenges
not a flower moves

delicate hands
ringing bells
i have not yet dared to hear
delicate hands
ringing bells
too high-pitched
for human ear

if even one petal moves
it will CATAPULT
me out of the desert
OUT OF THE DESERT!

but this is my home ———
this wandering
if even one petal moves ———

oh do not!

HAN GO NATSH AKAZUM TZEZERAK!

worse than caught
wanting to

all the rays prismatic
pinning the golden spider
against a netless jungle
of delicate flowers ———
without leaves

i don't even trust
the desert anymore

those damn flowers!

one petal
MUST MOVE!!

oh clown-hands
dance
dance like bells
in the desert
UNHEARD . . .

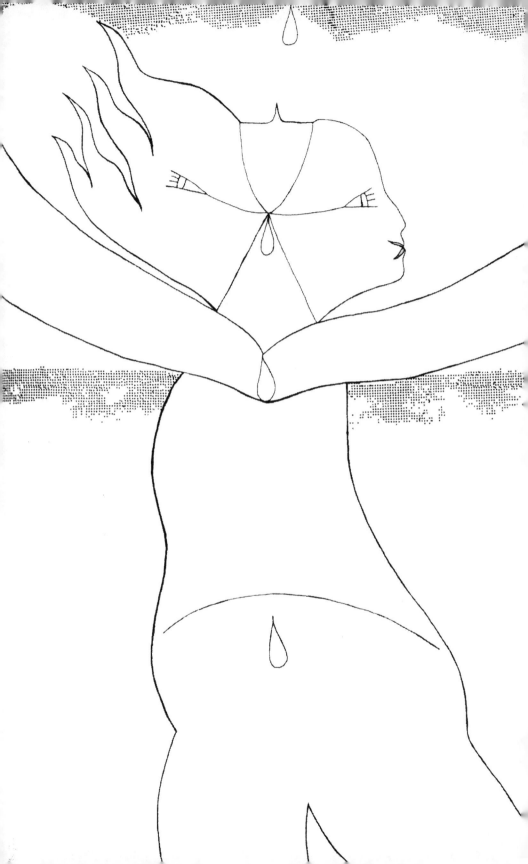

TWENTY-SECOND DAY

pain is the first step
into the desert

absence of pain
is the desert

not to have
is the desert

now to have where
is the desert

not to have where to dance
is the desert

the desert becomes dance

grain to grain
all colors
all pain the burning sand
the soul keeps moving
as soles of feet
on burning sand

twenty-two a double question mark
canceling perhaps
like a double negative
but is a question negative?

the noon-hot sun
flashes photo negative
all the structures
long erased
live strong in light of memory
while figures move against the dark
to mock

one must do something intelligent
don't know what
but something intelligent ———
like fast

grain to grain
all colors grin
all pain the burning sand
the soul keeps moving
as soles of feet
on burning sand

all the structures
long erased
live strong in light of memory
while figures mock against the dark

a chagall flying
defying gravity
and grave considerations

consider self

if one could know
the what to ask
it would be given

if one could let
the unknowing
free to feel its need
it could fill all on its own

if one could be
all on one's own
and never own a thing
and thus own all ———

but ifs are for the first step
into the desert

at twenty-two
it's all the way skidoo
gut-strings & feathers!

grain to grain
all colors
all pain the burning sand
the soul keeps moving
as soles of feet
on burning sand

if the dark forces come
what will you do?
twenty-two & skidoo?

when the dark forces come
i shall enter the heavy curtain
where cleopatra & mae west
trace lines & curves
against the wall

what curtain?
what wall?

when the dark forces are closer
i shall invoke the aid of
a ninety-seven-year-old patriarch
who was tied to his dying bed
to keep him from the last gesture

what man?
what bed?

when the dark forces are here
i shall call all the structures
long erased
and the figures within
and the figures without

i shall scream
for the double negative!

TWENTY-THIRD DAY

contact-points connected
shock more painful
than ever isolation
at the seethe of the vortex
no clear is possible
charged with all that power
all that knowing
and its continual annihilation ———
one must fly to the desert

one must fly to the desert
to sift
there
even the demons
lose their distortions
the great spread
releases
all the ballasts
the heart ———
vulnerable ———
takes each annihilation
back to life
pulsing

pages partial
must be ripped
out completely
with paper ———
quite possible

less so
the human heart
torn
hanging shreds obscene

a silent consonant
to guard
the unspeakable name
the color of blood
when light charges it
not red
and not
not red

the black man sometimes-blue
calling
she walks
she keeps on walking

the sweeper
in the ice-cream parlor
sweeps her into a sugar-cone
she keeps on walking
to cable the city

contact-points connected
shock more painful
than ever isolation
at the seethe of the vortex
no clear is possible
charged with all that power
all that knowing
and its continual annihilation ———
one must fly to the desert

she keeps on walking
to cable the city ———
rides one stop
past her past

a land
no one has ever seen ———
a land to ———
a land away from

to wobble footloose
in a sky just passing blue

angels baroque
struck horizontal
as directors
dos equis
two equal answers
in respective space
(not answering)

this is the land
that gobbled all the elements
first spaced by man
in his original division
of the universe
the first knowledge of four
extending vision
into space plus one

fable of fisherman & fish
whose wish
brought him before the shores of life ———
whose greed
decreed
his fall to his begin

once again
once must learn to wish
perhaps this time
one dares to ask
for more than possible

perhaps this time
one dares to ask
for love

TWENTY-FOURTH DAY

a structure in the desert
this time a chinese cement-box
lacquered to simulate wood

size enough
for any imaginable within

size enough
for any imagination
to be squashed

precision-rows of cabbages
the only green
a buzzer at the gate
i buzzed to ring the king

who's there?
a screech lacquered to simulate voice

me
would you spare some water?

a buzzard flew by
the wings lacquered
clacking a simulate-laughter

back to sand
back to the sand-dance
back to catch
thoughts like flies
swarm in the sun
glisten the night
ageless night-dance
that knows no home
only gives of itself
to extreme

a tent went up
a spiderweb in the desert
caught sun as rainbow
through tears

insects came to investigate
could make no head or tail of it
they went through
were not caught

a few went far enough to ask
what's it for?
will it fly?

a voice answered
someone left their pants last night

a voice answered
she's wonderful when incoherent

heard my own voice burning
against the sun
GIVE ME A REASON TO LIVE!

a tawny spider whispered
whoops! almost

sefardic mexican-blue
a SHOFAR sounded once
DUNCE!
FIND A REASON TO DIE!

a minute white spider
landed on my arm
fixing me squarely
with bright black eyes ———
his face a square
white mask
mouth moving
a mime
no sound
calliope music

a SHOFAR sounded twice
DOUBLE YOUR TROUBLE
DIVIDE IT BY TWO

sefardic mexican-blue

once fly crawled away sighing
i go to sleep all the time
i don't know what's the matter with me

a SHOFAR sounded thrice
LIVE OR DIE
OR ENTER VICE

the tent began to rock
slowly gathering momentum
names started dropping
like falling stars
fell to pattern
only a child alone
in the night
AWAKE
could bounce into
and onto a jump-and-bounce
night-call

all the children
jumping the night-pattern
all over the world

each alone
awake at night
bouncing the night-pattern

YOU GOT TO GIVE
WITHOUT WANTING TO GET
TO LEARN RECEIVING

the tent went
it was all butterfly-wings
threaded
no flies caught like thoughts
no thoughts at all

only the membrane
of each fly
caught
swarm against the sun
glisten the night
ageless night-dance
that knows no home
only gives of itself
to extreme

Labs 842 74.01 76

TWENTY-FIFTH DAY

sheer here
on spun glass walking ————
the thread a-quiver
a quiver filled with arrows
about to be shot

this is the desert
sweets!
the moments are one's own
but heaven help the one
who dares defy the line

the line as in the devil
as the circle is to god
the circle is a line
returning

without a line
there would be no circle

insanity
definition:
the script thrown away
without a plot!

outside the story
the gory details gone
without a plot
to piss in

without a plot!
without a song
without the gong
at dinner-time

outside the circle-sound
to bring one home

no oasis!
no pond
no pebble into
to circle out

the still will stands a-quiver
a quiver filled with arrows
about to be shot

the perserverated possibilities
are endless

a perforated arch-board
floats just above the sand
without a single mark
to mar the bullseye

her long dark hair
circles a face
as if masked
circus-clown-white

the eyes lidded
a-quiver silver
a quiver filled with arrows
about to be shot

she feels her indian strong
but the indian is not pure
so she's not sure
what is her right
and what is her wrong

some worcester, please!

without a plot
the story has a chance
to make it
on its own

some worcester, please!

city-sounds
a pebble in
a pond
to circle out

but this is the desert
sweets!
the moments are one's own
but heaven help the one
who dares defy the line

so much horizon on the desert!

where is the sign
to force this line
into direction?

some worcester, please!

if one remains long enough
still enough ———
one arrow is bound to ———
except like X
one is forced
by animal nature
of preservation
to move constantly
from the point
where one line
crosses the other

the perserverated possibilities
are endless

a perforated arch-board
floats just above the sand
an arrow
struck in its
bullseye

TWENTY-SIXTH DAY

you can't make a bad move
unless you got a bad motive!

myself that spoke
a long ago longing
that knowing still only words
not yet meshed
into the being

poet bill put the words
upon his wheel
spokes spinning
to flash it clear

the wheel is warming
to your question
ask!
ask what you have not dared
to ask

you can't make a bad move
unless you got a bad motive!
yet why does the world
do me so foolish?

spokes spinning
to flash it clear
you are the world
you are yet foolish

who spoke?
myself that spoke?

disorder demands
utmost efficiency
just as what seems to flounder
falls easily
into its rightful place

you can't make a bad move
unless you got a bad motive!

and mother asked
if she could give the movers lunch
hell no! answered the daughter
i'm paying them by the hour

illusion comes to taunt
in any form desire sparks
in the desert
it is water
in an oasis
it is a visitor ———
a someone
a something
anything for contact

perhaps a fly
rubbing its legs
and if the tiny features
show a mouth moving
what depth of conversation
could ensue!

but there is not even one fly
it is time for the ghostly visitor
like a slow door closing
in a place that knows no door
only the change
too vast
too fast
for human belief

the ghostly visitor insists
it has something to teach
i strain to it
therefore cannot learn it

it is precisely that
that must be learned

instead only
the knock knock
no one there
only a clutter
and a clatter
a space jammed
with the most unsightly sounds

did i call that?
it must be so
or it would not be so
how to be rid of all that
in me?

the path must be cleared
before light can enter
the spokes must be clean
before the wheel can flash clear

the room was tall
on many levels
every day the windows widened
the levels kept changing
as more & more light entered
until one day
the room was gone

not even one fly
rubbing its legs
on even one window-pane

no window
no room

it is terrible
to be given just a glimpse ———
to know the terrible shining ———
a toe caught in the slamming door

i didn't hear a door slam
didn't even know
there was a door

the levels kept changing
as more & more light entered

and one day
the room is gone

no window
no room

only ———

ONLY ALL LIGHT!

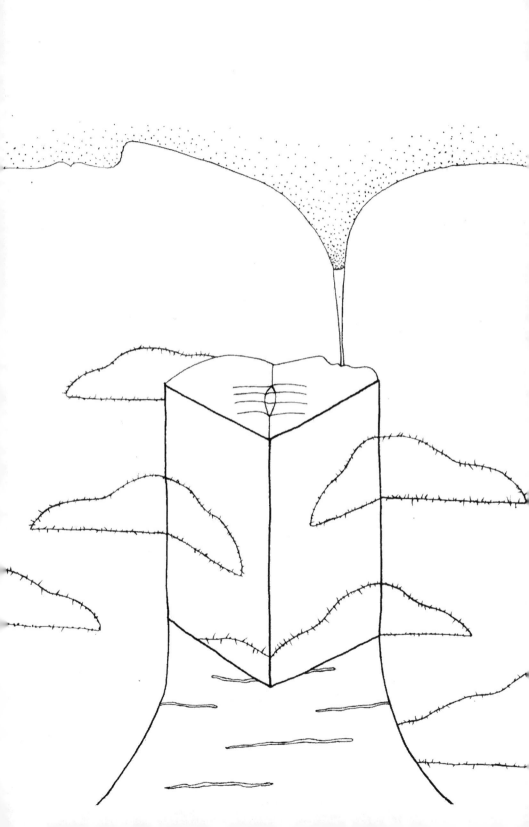

TWENTY-SEVENTH DAY

from yearning-peak
to yearning-peak
an angel streaks
a rush of wings
barely brushing
its cycle against the foot of the horizon

KALPA!

moth-circle
the wheel in the structure
a warning
and a confirmation

from out of the past
come the questions
one has to tread softly
not to shatter illusion
all at once

in that instant
boulders are born
to roll wild & measured
against the foot of the horizon

still they are only of sand
and sly
no nearer to the goal

only enough of a change
to give a kick to the quick
a put-on high
a depth in a flat flat yearning

the tentacles of a mad world
still root
in the chambers
of a divided heart

what land
have you yet to teach?

not one
that cannot be guessed

not one
to make guest
of the stranger

still you overwhelm
permit the boomerang
that splits laughing

you who knows so well
your clowns
upon the glacial landscape
the desert on the verge of birth

monsters of innocence
chatter incessant & soundless

and what seems to arrive
is on the point of departure

crystals flashed
causing a name
and the name
brought it down
yet the name allowed
the departure-point to flow

KALPA!

moth-circle
the wheel in the structure
a warning
and a confirmation

blue is a color
blue is a sound
blue ranged unhindered
cold & soft

red is a color
red is a sound
red cannot range
having committed itself

words beyond meaning
sounds beyond words
silence beyond sound
the gesture charged
a mime on a desert stage
electric the wings
swooping against the foot of the horizon

white is a color
white is all color
white ranges unhindered
yet committed

NO SOUL!
RUN FOR YOUR LIFE!

the mime raises his desert foot

I DO NOT ASK
I QUESTION

sand trickles down
from between the toes
of the desert-clown

I DON'T WANT MORE GAMES!
I WANT TO BE RID OF THE GAMES I KNOW!

the foot of the mime
is still raised & unmoving

I QUIT

the foot plunks down
a spray of sand
the mime is vanished

KALPA!

a white feather
floats from yearning-peak
to yearning-peak
against the foot of the horizon

TWENTY-EIGHTH DAY

so this is the desert
beyond the desert ————
one is too dry even to cry
one is out of reach
even to screech
there are no stops
and no horizon
there is no path
there is no lie
left to lie upon
there is no up
there is no on
there is not even down

it is not too hot
it is not too cold
there is no old
no feet to walk
no hands to hold
and nothing in-between

it does not hurt
and it does not not hurt
for pain can only come with joy

fear & fingers & all the things
that linger
like rain
are not here now
to make someone feel again

if memory
is the toy of joy
and equally pain
TEAR OUT
the tongue of bells
hell to rhyme
must follow
as star about its given
and unasked for

for someone knows
no one
for someone
is permitted
pitted
to each
of its own monsters

someone accepts
beyond the desert
where too dry to cry
too out of reach
to screech

no stops
and no horizon
the eye upon
no path
no lie
left to lie upon
no up
no on
no even down

TWENTY-NINTH DAY

utter peace ————
a calm that stretches
beyond the sound of horizon
the sound of colors
broken to its utmost molecule

it is not safe here ————
nor even sweet

to cut through all the shit ————
to cut it fine
so fine
only time will ————
finer than sand
sieved as a child will
pretending cookery

as the princess & the pea
and all those tales of sensitivity

in the desert
where no water to flush
only the crush of sun
and the hope of night
which comes late
and too cold to take ————
is that possibility

when i lived around here
i used to go there
now that there is here
i go to where was there

a cat's cradle huge-strung in the sky
the game the same as in a child's hands

oh fevers sweet
a boat a cradle
on a sparkling rocking sea
darted with monsters
playful shine & darkly

it happened
CRASH!
the thought done
the tune hung in mid-air
a cat's cradle huge-strung in the sky
a dead girl suspended
a sacrifice to light
the light that shone through the girl
the web the thought
that happened

that tired dog
my body dreams & whimpers
don't stand up!
someone might know you
left body & died
is it that easy?
that carcass shed
no more involving me
in its illusions

gloated one thought too long
cost me a lifetime
and there i was in it again

oh to break the pattern
as sand breaks its pattern

could cry
but tears are not easy
in the desert
hardly possible

there were sweated out long ago
through many a delirium

oh fevers sweet
a boat a cradle
on a sparkling rocking sea
darted with monsters
playful shine & darkly

and all the friendly faces
family portraits
a thousand more miniatures
suspended on invisible threads
to swing in
an army of memories all threat

even the desert
cannot completely
halt this sea of eyes
breaking over these mouths
changing each mouth
a language
a sound unique cry of grief
of joy relief
of alive
and all that moves with it

i reach
a grain of sand brutal waves

BE NOT DECEIVED!
LEAVE ALL THAT IS DEAR!
THE RETURN IS NOT YOURS
FOR THE ASKING

the red sea in a woodrose
beads of light
in the night-sweat of cities fevered
what would a rose
if red only?

rose before dawn
left with bread unrisen

across the sea that opened
a virgin path

THIRTIETH DAY

as sound rebounds
the slightest obstacle
so does it give lie
to the desert
the doppelgänger giggles
behind each grain of sand ———
does not even bother to mask
the odd & even balanced
against itself
cancels

the best one can do
is to invite the devil to tea
you may not need lemon
you may not need cream
but hope that you need enough
to be able to scream
ABEL is dead
and his brother pays the dues
ABEL is dead ———
guess who sings the blues

it's less than a guess
and more than a grain
a voice pitched & angled
like fish at an intersection
who is shark more than
trout with bones
numberless tones
stuck in one's throat

there are numbers like birds
struck with fire like feather
both ends burning
as the game starts playing

a kid could
as any old goat
say cheese
please all your elders
and up your elder tree

and the man
whose wife did him in
burnt all the trees
in his orchard
he had so carefully tended
during his shipping-trips home

the best one can do
is to invite the devil to tea
you may not need lemon
you may not need cream
but hope that you need enough
to be able to scream
ABEL is dead
and his brother pays the dues
ABEL is dead ———
guess who sings the blues

back water back
crack earth crack!

do not tremble in the desert
je suis responsible

crack enough
for one ant to leave

all the antennae
are one ant
all relation
is one sister & one brother
related to one father
and one mother

the line is fine
one fable to touch
one grandmother
is sheer harem cloth
to tell one story
once more

MAKE A HOLE IN A BIRD
FOR THE SKY!

THIRTY-FIRST DAY

the city of oneself
crawls over the desert
looking for solid ground

this creature
from the AAGH or UR
lured
into the lurid bright

once upon a time
all creatures were blind

once upon a time ———

since the wheel
there is no invention

a wheel spins
just above the sand

its space cuts
the city-wall

a glass shriek!
an eye-crash
open

THIRTY-SECOND DAY

A

VOID

CANNOT

BE

AVOIDED

THIRTY-THIRD DAY

when it rains in the desert
it rains
limbo-gray the day
the rain keeps pouring

the only warmth is fever
galloping relentless hooves of tears
the leave one tearless
rocked with dry dry laughter

haunched oriental
one makes oneself into a tent
hover over one small flame
trying to keep it dry

two parallel matches
headed in opposite directions
burnt out
waiting to be devoured
by the living flame
one hovers over
trying to keep dry

there is no warmth in that flame
the only warmth is fever
galloping relentless hooves of tears
that leave one tearless
rocked with dry dry laughter

and in that laughter
between each rock
of yes god yes god
i know god
oh how i must know
not knowing it yet

using i
and not using your name
in vain
ADONOI

and in that laughter
between each rock

not a rock
not even a pebble
upon which to focus

and in that laughter
between each rock
one small flame endures

the vision of man
the game that is man

the childhood
of running & stop stop
look & listen
where did all the others go?

the first friend
that joy of touch & go
how did it go now?
when did it went?
was it circumstance or time
a rhyme to keep it
just a little longer ...

perhaps a train ———
a wet & waving handkerchief
white & bright in the night
while steam & soot
etched root into the heart

pulsed perhaps a ship
that took a trip
never to return

now the rain makes desert into sea
black & stuck with memory

hover over one small flame
to try to keep it dry

and in that laughter
between each rock
the lover appears
to disappear again & again
taking all forms & giving back
only an image
the lover who much reach you
in such pain
that gain is loss
and toss upon a desert sea

and in that laughter
between each rock
the lover who is now
the moment that all the others paled
a light so bright
that one small flame
could never be hover
but stand up straight in the rain
and all the rain
could never douse that flame
nor even the matches that lit it
could ever be symbol

opposite headed
burnt out
waiting to be devoured
by the living flame

could never be symbol enough

not that simply!

THIRTY-FOURTH DAY

after the storm
a great sigh
sweeps the land
even the desert responds ———
the desert
that accepts all & shrugs

the sand cakes
makes the wind work
the wanderer moves even more slowly
it is easier
to put one foot
in front of the other
it is more possible
to cross another being
and no desert-wanderer is ever
quite willing to encourage this
that yearning
is kept quite secret ———
a secret so open
only those who would enter this realm
could
and they do
unlikely currents
do draw
the most solid & temporary contacts

in the desert
suddenly a structure
turns out to be a walk-around-ceiling

mother would not be able to move into it
yet it was mother
who found it

yes
says the little-girl manager ———
only bare necessities ———
only bare necessities ———
a window
a bed
a closet perhaps
a chair
maybe even a table

a flash struck the lovers!
the were separate
in their identical awareness

one was bound
to return to claim it ———
hold with sweat-slip-hand
the life-cord
dropped
from the walk-around-ceiling

not being blind
has a high price ———
forced to see
forced to relate
forced to act ———
even to inflicting of pain
on others ———
the fiercest pain yet
even to being seen as weak
even to not being seen

there is a vanishing point in grief
there is a vanishing point in self
the wanderer moves even more slowly ...
even as that one
seems to accelerate

the desert too real
vanishes in mirage

the mask is triangle
all sharp & cornered ———
a grin on the mime features ———
a dancer moves

feet trace on the wet-caked sand:

I MUST BE ALONE!
I DON'T WANT TO BE ALONE!
I AM ALONE
BONE TO SAND ...

hands trace on the steam-tracked air:

LEAVE THE PATH OF THE FATHER!
LEAVE THE PATH OF THE MOTHER!

and the mask is triangle
all sharp & cornered ———
a grin on the mime features ———
a dancer stops to vanish

the structure shrugs into sand

the walk-around-ceiling was your idea
so you're struck with it
without a structure

no self-respecting mirage
would accept that

the wanderer cannot even blame the desert

if he turns to tent
or becomes content
for as long as
one is to realize
for as long as
one can see ———
who would be better?

the way of the blind?
the way of the kind?

be as the wind
having to work
to make the wet sand move

try not so hard
to be hard
or stone
or bone
but better yet
leave only the skull
to transmit one message
to be found
by that wanderer
who would only see the skull
and never lure the soul
from its source

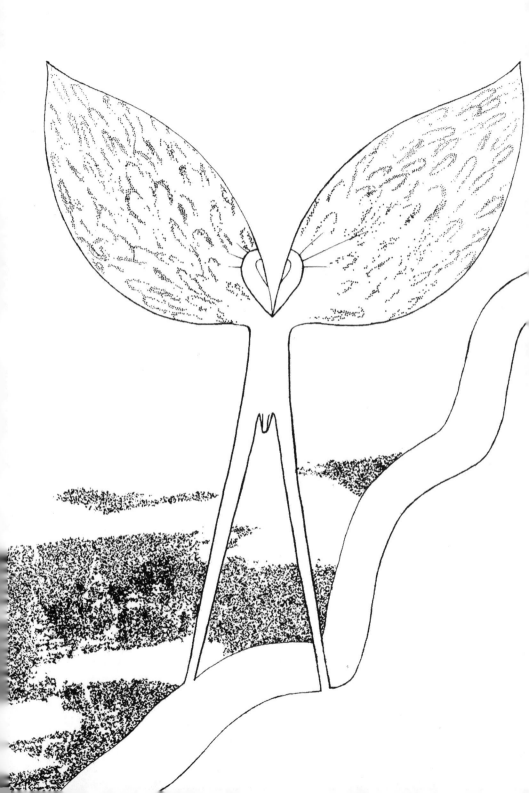

THIRTY-FIFTH DAY

the next oasis must be avoided
the ground might be fertile enough
for roots

thirst is not the worst
in the desert

into this shape
without meaning ——— to ———

but meant
as lent a mask
to borrow another

maybe at first
of father or mother
or friend

the trend could be dangerous

but that too is optional

How real is i?
how feel the sky?

the beasts that roam the desert
are a rare breed
to one another ————

like lovers!

THIRTY-SIXTH DAY

so OK
let go!
LET GO!
lettie go
lotte-lenya-let-go
now let go now
NOW!
LET GO!

ho
no season or reason
or watch what you say
it may trounce you but good
oh lady be good
are you good, lady?
are you a ——— good lady?
ARE YOU GOOD! LADY!
are you ——— a lady?
ARE YOU GOOD???

all romantic inclination
is a likely hill
in the desert ———
which the wind deems to shift
like feel a lift ———
you wouldn't wear a skirt
in the desert ———
a long shirt will do

if the lady has a husband
she cane use HIS
like sugarcane can
or hers is worse
for not being worn ————
her virginity
oh divinity
torn out of blood
the flood!

why get a room in a hotel
when all will tell anyway?

william tell
shot his apple
in the squarest
most bank-yet-country
and came up arrow through

eve & apple-up your sleeve
american way
APPLE PAN DOWDY
you hear that?
DOWDY!
that's an american word
i think
THINK
you might like the change
jingle
on your sweet pringle
and dowdy
who's boston enough
to know it now?

in the new moon
the energy must be won once more
the desert ponders the wanderer
as the wanderer panders the desert
does a panderer ponder the desert?
does a panderer pander?
a pimp for soul
is the true monarch butterfly
whores in the orient
wear butterflies

can it truly be so simple?

each cocoon
a moon like new wine
maroon-colored wine
for the soul
and white for the hope
that turned it liquid
loose enough
to hope for some small scope

so OK
let go!
LET GO!
let tongue thick & all
black & plague
but that's another day
when one hits the cities
so OK
LET GO!

THIRTY-SEVENTH DAY

would you believe?
would you believe
the itch in your ear?
would you believe
even when there is nothing?

how to relieve
the weight of fate & mind?
the mind that monsters
methodical beads
inscribed with hieroglyphs
of that most ancient tale
called love

seven beads ———
seven is the number of my life
three is the number of my love
and it came in the night
a flashlight
and four from my life
a flash of light
like a gun in the hand
from my steps in the sand
it must be he
who else but that firethief
who the gods are after
in this life
and the many before
four from my life
WHO? WHO? WHO?
not you!
not from me!
it couldn't be!

to a new love
flash & crystal
who is death
breath from life
to an old true love
the rue love
on the street of tears
beads methodical as crystals

in a half-message
where one is about to roll into a ball
to die
on the thirty-seventh day
in the desert
which could be ten
read (or blue)
could be ten
read another way ———
the way is always open
in the desert ———
red & blue
makes magenta
the magnetic color of soul ———
in a half-message
understood just enough
to be misunderstood

MISS UNDERSTOOD
studied her part well
she never knew
where her turn to enter would
and entertain her game
to detain fact enough from fiction
to cause friction
a spark in the dark yearning
to burn filthy clean
a churn of lovers

lovers to remain lovers
must conjure
the most barren desert
for each other ————
themselves having already
put themselves there

now there is not where
the lone upon the desert would ————
but there is where
each must
as new wine
drunk in the autumn
in the color of leaves falling

fall ———— fall
do not fear to fall

would you believe
even when there is nothing?

but there is where
for here is four stolen beads
hieroglyphed & stoned
to an ancient tale
and like the reflection
of black on the back
of someone in front of light ————
so those purloined beads
were simply a joke of fate
for the sake of change
des enfants terribles
those children pranksters
who not knowing
what they do
give the most terrible present
called NOW
for a to come
called YES

would you believe
the waters came
to extinguish
the hate of fate & mind ————
when all the messenger-demons
sent by the gods
after this firethief
came to do me in?

would you believe
even when there is nothing
left to believe in?

never
but why not
end with a preposition!

THIRTY-EIGHTH DAY

the worst in the desert
is not thirst
the worst in the desert
in not the vast
it is the poe pit
without the pendulum
it is the poe pendulum
without the pit

and so one carries
illusion of substance
be it pain or gain
and so one carries
the contact further
causing more pain & more gain ———
knowing it is only illusion
one even calls it love ———
creates a pit with a pendulum
creates a pendulum with a pit

and the pendulum swings
and the pit worms one further
into the dark

a night like any other
a day all day
send-thoughts have burned & burned
through night through day

one becomes monolithic

the egyptians knew the word
when they burned the jews
in their mortar-sun
forced the run through
a red sea
through a bloody eye
live or die
but one must try!
woe to the one
who will not
whose will
is burned to the mortar sun

one becomes monolithic

the greeks went myth
and the blond hair of the father
became the black eye of the mother

there is a finnish tale
that it is dark
three in a room drinking ———
SKOL & SHALOM ———
the finn wins in losing
sez
ARE WE DRINKING OR TALKING???

walking on rocks
that is sand with the sea

irish tales
little people dancing
dancing on the graves
of those who wish they were dead
but never can be
they would not live it out
long enough to stop the scrimmage
the image of one's being

the worst in the desert
is not thirst
the worst in the desert
is not the vast
it is the illusion of substance

france where the girls
without pants
(rumor unconfirmed)
knew in its frog-being
only seed-beads strung & strung
on the female clung to ———

one cannot orient oneself
to a universe flashing
sunset sunrise simultaneous

the desert asks that
only that
what wanderer
would dare that challenge?
and the cold stars too ———
knowing it is only illusion
one even calls it love

the pendulum swings
the pendulum struck
and swung with blood
bells boomed & rang

IT IS OVER

IT IS OVER

IT IS OVER

through a red sea
through a bloody eye
live or die
but one must try!

and one could lie no more
and die

AND IT IS SHALOM!

THIRTY-NINTH DAY

falling
falling
fighting air

space cuts
an echo of whispers

FEEL OUT   OUT
FEEL IN
LET SIN   GO ———————————

no more must
the rusty hinge of past
unhinged

falling
falling
free

there is time to look now!
look
LET SIN   GO ———————————

and what is in?
and what is sin?

sand-grains whisper
rush into each other
wind has consented
play slow
there is time to look now!

sand sands sand
bumps away laughing

wings
dark things hover
cover the desert
as far as the eye cannot see
waiting waiting
for an open wound

wind is a higher game

and the wanderer who has fallen
to feel once more
sits on his butt
having hit hard
legs spread away
head still spinning

wings
dark things hover
cover the desert
as far as the eye cannot see

and the wanderer gazes dazed
at his open wounds closing

wings
dark things change shape
move not up
but away

wings
warning
as they swarm away
a shrill flight & slow

THE RETURN
IS YOURS FOR THE ASKING

ask any king ————
his queen plays cards
and tells it all
but he must touch
his house of cards
and see it fall

little girl
leave your doll
she has told you
all she knows

little boy
take off your flying clothes
you can fly
without them

the worst in the desert
is not thirst
the worst in the desert
is not the vast
the worst in the desert
is the past

come pit
come pendulum
do me in!

LET GO SIN

all of me
part of me
none of me

LET GO SIN

FEEL OUT   OUT
FEEL IN

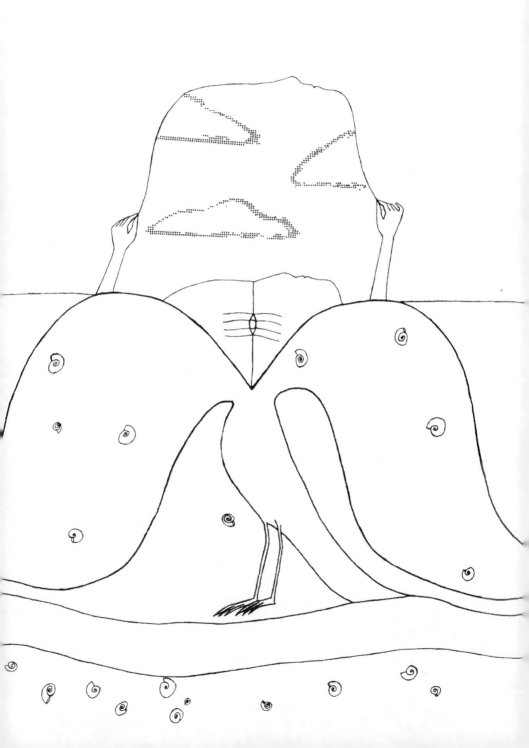

FORTIETH DAY

how does one start
what one has to finish?

a hard line?
a fine line?
a blurred edge
into another self?

a gull screeches
scraping the universe

a bird?
A GULL!!!
the sea must be near!

the desert become dear
the desert become home
the desert forcing alone
is about to desert
the wanderer to another fate
where perhaps to relate
is even more painful

a feather on sand ...
the foot has stopped
as has the other
a hand reaches down
fingers & feather ...

was such a funny bird
turned & turned
wouldn't fly away

are you not a unicorn?
no! he said
i have two horns

lighter than light
he padded the sand
said ——— where i land
you must follow

sound of wings
crossed the current of things
and i blurred ———

i? ——— blurred?

blurred like a bird

humming-birds
flowers & honey

a house is to live inside

sound of own voice
makes quiver
and shiver & quail
frail tone
strong as longing
bone & marrow
bone to arrow
lighter than light

it hurts
it hurts
it hurts
to leave the desert
it hurts

FOUR TIMES!

forty
thieves came to her tent
leaving olive-leaves
they shouldered the gold
and started back
across the desert

the tent went
it was all wings & leaves
in the wind

and she on the edge
blurred & fine & hard

an outline against the sea
hard & fine & blurred

she'd sprout wings
maybe talk about things
to that funny bird
that turned & turned
wouldn't fly away

she touched one horn
it was of the sea
she touched the other
it was of the land

and twin-spirals propelled her
lighter than light

Photo by Christopher Felver, 2007

About ruth weiss

ruth weiss is one of the last living significant poets of
the Beat Generation. Born to a Jewish family during
the rise of Nazism, she eventually made her way to the
United States where she became friends with, and a
contemporary of, the likes of Jack Kerouac and many
other artists of the 1950s American counter-culture
movement of San Francisco (specifically in North
Beach). In the 1960s she began spelling her name in
lowercase letters in a symbolic protest against "law
and order" since in her birthplace of Germany all nouns
are capitalized. She continues to perform live in North
Beach and at many jazz and poetry festivals around the
world. In this age of high-speed information exchange,
she still uses her "Loyal Royal" metal typewriter,
and lives deep in the Northern California forests of
Mendocino County, USA.

About the Artist

Paul Blake

Born in New York City, May 16, 1945, the artist Paul Blake graduated in 1965 from Chouinard Art Institute in Los Angeles where he studied with Emerson Woelffer and Robert Irwin. His work has been widely exhibited on the West Coast and is included in private collections in New York City, Chicago, Los Angeles, Seattle, San Francisco, Mexico City, and Jerusalem. He has prepared numerous covers and drawings for magazines and books of poetry. Of the present work, he writes, "The drawings are moments—places—'rememberings' of inner journey parallel with (but not illustrative of) *DESERT JOURNAL*, a work I have lived with, heard aloud often and watched grow for some years—complete and separate onto themselves, yet connected from the core, the source of their becoming."

HERSTORY

1949. hitch-hiked from CHICAGO to NEW YORK. on
to NEW ORLEANS in 1950. where at 22 i was first
published in issues of BRUCE LIPPINCOTT'S THE OLD
FRENCH QUARTER NEWS. had jammed with musicians at
the ART CIRCLE. where i lived in CHICAGO in 1949. but
it was in NEW ORLEANS that the repartee between my
voice & the riffs of bebop reached a deeper dimension.
BRUCE on sax. JOHNNY ELGIN on keyboard. other
musicians joined the jam.

the word TIMING is my major guideline. in performance.
in my daily life. so it is fitting that DESERT JOURNAL
published in 1977 by GOOD GAY POETS in BOSTON is
now reprinted in NEW ORLEANS. the city i left in 1951.

this is my first return in 2012. by invitation. not only
for a stroll down memory lane. but a show & tell. of the
poem that is my life. as it continues.

thank you DAVID BRINKS for finding the thread &
winding that thread to pull me in.

———ruth weiss

DESERT JOURNAL HAS A LIFE OF ITS OWN

a life of its own — this book DESERT JOURNAL.
thought it would be novel to write a novel.
do the math. 5 x 4 = 200. so for 40 days do 5 pages.

decision. 5 pages non-stop each day whatever
surfaces. even if only one word per page. forget
characters & plot. this is a novel moderne.

focus — the internal desert. being a water-sign — most
fearful place the desert. need to explore that place.
had never been to the actual desert.

1961. begin. it was finished in 1968. 7 years.

readings through those years had audience call
numbers up to the point of completion. someone would
always ask "how do you know this about me?" DESERT
JOURNAL has a life of its own. i'm only the instrument.

sent manuscript out. no takers. 1975. went to NEW
YORK CITY. in & out of publishing houses. no takers.
back home in SAN FRANCISCO. no mistaking the
message. MAGNETIZE THE CALL FOR IT.

a week later. phone call from BOSTON. CHARLEY
SHIVELY of GOOD GAY POETS press. had heard me at
WILD SIDE WEST, a women's bar in SAN FRANCISCO. i
had mentioned looking for a publisher.

DESERT JOURNAL came out in 1977. currently i've
stolen lines from it & collaged into new poems — LIGHT
WORKS, BYPASS LINZ, & SUICIDE DREAMS.

40 days — 7 years. those numbers have far-reaching
biblical references. was not aware of that.

now, thanks to DAVID BRINKS of TREMBLING PILLOW
press in NEW ORLEANS, this book continues as a
reprint. on a life of its own.

———ruth weiss

Acknowledgements:

Some of the days of *DESERT JOURNAL* have appeared in *Panjandrum Poetry 2 & 3* (1973), *This is Women's Work* (1974), *Room* (1976), *Heirs Magazine No. 11* (1976), *Reconstructing the Beats* (2004), *Breaking the Rule of Cool* (2004), and *Translaciones. Poetas traductores 1939 - 1959* (2012). *DESERT JOURNAL* was first published in 1977 in hardback and paperback editions by Good Gay Poets, Boston.

Music for *Fortieth Day* was composed by Gerhard Samuel for soprano, spoken voice, oboe, alto saxophone, violin, cello, keyboard and percussion — first performance December 13th, 1976 Monday Evening Concerts at the Los Angeles County Museum of Art with the poet voicing and the composer conducting.

Images on the cover and in the text used by permission of the artist, Paul Blake.

Bibliography of ruth weiss

BOOKS

STEPS (1958)
GALLERY OF WOMEN (1959)
SOUTH PACIFIC (1959)
BLUE IN GREEN (1960)
LIGHT and other poems (1976)
DESERT JOURNAL (1977)
SINGLE OUT (1978)
13 HAIKU (1986)
FOR THESE WOMEN OF THE BEAT (1997)
A NEW VIEW OF MATTER (1999)
FULL CIRCLE (2002)
AFRICA (2003)
WHITE IS ALL COLORS (2004)
NO DANCING ALOUD (2006)
CAN'T STOP THE BEAT: The Life and Words of a Beat
Poet (2011)

VIDEO AUDIO FILM CD:

THE BRINK
originally 16mm, 40 min., b &w, 1961, video
1986

POETRY & ALL THAT JAZZ volume 1
audio & video, live performance with
Doug O'Conner-bass, with acoustic bass
accompaniment (1990)

POETRY & ALL THAT JAZZ volume 2
audio, performance with Larry Vukovich- piano
Omar Clay- drums, Ilse Eckinger-bass, Live
performance with jazz trio (1993)

A NEW VIEW OF MATTER
CD, live performance with Matthias von
Hintzenstern- cello, mouth-harp, overtone voice
(2000)

JAZZ FEST BERLIN
CD, Live performance with Gerhard Graml-acoustic bass, Friedrich Legerer- sax, Stefan Brodsky- percussion (2000)

JAZZ GRABENFEST VIENNA (DREI FARBEN WEISS)
CD, live performance with Achim Tang- acoustic bass, Boris Hauf- sax, Lukas Knofler- drums, (2004)

TURNABOUT
CD, recording with Hal Davis- percussion, Thomas Shoemaker-electric guitar, (2010)

FILMS BY STEVEN ARNOLD WITH ruth weiss IN MAJOR ROLES

LIBERATION OF MANNIQUE MECHANIQUE (1967)
16mm, b & w

THE VARIOUS INCARNATIONS OF A TIBETAN SEAMSTRESS (1967)
16mm, b & w

MESSAGES, MESSAGES (1968)
16mm b & w

LUMINOUS PROCURESS (1971)
35mm, color

PYRAMID (1972)
16mm, b & w

OTHER FILMS

THE RISE AND FALL OF THE WORLD AS SEEN FROM A SEXUAL POSITION, dir. Arthur Meyer (1972)

LAS CUEVAS DE ALBION (2002) b & w and color, live performance with Tao Ruspoli-flamenco guitar

BREAKING THE RULES (documentary) (2005),
dir. Angie Josefina Koch, NEUZEITFILM

IBÉRIA (2006), dir. Eddy Falconer

ruth weiss meets her prometheus (documentary)
(2007), dir. Frederik Baker

ARTWORK

poem prints (broadsides) with the author's
artwork
serigraphs by Paul Blake with the author's poetry
one woman exhibits of haiku paintings

COLLECTIONS

Author's work is included in Private, University &
Public Library Collections in U. S. & Europe
Most comprehensive collection at the Bancroft
Library University of California, Berkeley

PLAYS PRODUCED

THE 61ST YEAR TO HEAVEN (1961)
B NATURAL (1961, 1973, 1988)
M & M (1961, 1965)
MISPRINTS (1961, 1965)
NO DANCING ALOUD (1962, 1972, 1973, 2006)
FIGS (1965, 1988, 2006)
THE THIRTEEN WITCH (1983)
ONE KNIGHT + ONE DAY (2006)

OTHER PLAYS

LATE ONE EARLY
MEDIA—MEDIUM
SHOES
STOP THAT FLOWER
TWO PLAYERS & FIVE PLAYERS

FORTIETH DAY from DESERT JOURNAL was set to music for instruments, soprano and the spoken voice by Gerhard Samuel, with the composer conducting and the poet voicing. It premiered at the Monday Evening Concerts at the Los Angeles Museum of Art in 1976.

In 1994, the San Francisco Main Library presented a retrospective exhibit of work created by ruth weiss and Paul Blake over a period of 25 years.

In 2004, was awarded a bronze medal for literary achievement from Vienna, Austria.

Titles from Trembling Pillow Press

I of the Storm by Bill Lavender
Olympia Street by Michael Ford
Ethereal Avalanche by Gina Ferrara
Transfixion by Bill Lavender
The Ethics of Sleep by Bernadette Mayer
DOWNTOWN by Lee Meitzen Grue
SONG OF PRAISE Homage to John Coltrane (with CD)
by John Sinclair
Untitled Writings from a Member of the Blank Generation
by Philip Good
DESERT JOURNAL by ruth weiss (reprint)

Forthcoming Titles:

Aesthesia Balderdash by Kim Vodicka
Maniac Memories by Jim Gustafson
Full Tilt Boogie or What's the Point by Paul Chasse

Trembling
Pillow
PRESS
www.tremblingpillowpress.com